Novels for Students, Volume 40

Project Editor: Sara Constantakis Rights Acquisition and Management: Leitha Etheridge-Sims, Tracie Richardson Composition: Evi Abou-El-Seoud Manufacturing: Rhonda Dover

Imaging: John Watkins

Product Design: Pamela A. E. Galbreath, Jennifer Wahi Content Conversion: Katrina Coach Product Manager: Meggin Condino © 2012 Gale, Cengage Learning

For product information and technology assistance, contact us at **Gale Customer Support, 1-800-877-4253.**

For permission to use material from this text or product, submit all requests online at **www.cengage.com/permissions**.

Further permissions questions can be emailed to **permissionrequest@cengage.com** While every effort has been made to ensure the reliability of the information presented in this publication, Gale, a part of Cengage Learning, does not guarantee the accuracy of the data contained herein. Gale accepts no payment for listing; and inclusion in the publication of any organization, agency, institution, publication, service, or individual does not imply endorsement of the editors or publisher. Errors brought to the attention of the publisher and verified to the satisfaction of the publisher will be corrected in future editions.

Gale
27500 Drake Rd.
Farmington Hills, MI, 48331-3535

ISBN-13: 978-1-4144-8538-6
ISBN-10: 1-4144-8538-7
ISSN 1094-3552

This title is also available as an e-book.

ISBN-13: 978-1-4144-8231-6
ISBN-10: 1-4144-8231-0
Contact your Gale, a part of Cengage Learning sales
representative for ordering information.

Printed in Mexico
1 2 3 4 5 6 7 16 15 14 13 12

The Road

CORMAC McCARTHY

2006

INTRODUCTION

Cormac McCarthy's *The Road*, published in 2006, is a work of dystopian fiction about a man and his son struggling for survival in a postapocalyptic world. An unnamed catastrophe has wiped out almost all life on earth. Most of the few humans who remain have given up any notion of moral decency and have become cannibals who travel in packs hunting for people to enslave, murder, and eat. The man's overwhelming love for his son and his desire to protect him are the only things that sustain him in this horrifying world. Many critics of the work have speculated that it was inspired by McCarthy's own son John Francis, who was around the same age as the boy in the novel at the time of its publication. The inscription in the front of the book dedicates the work to his son.

Although the setting of the story is never specified, it seems likely that it takes place in the United States sometime in the future. No proper nouns are used in the work: no places, or people, are ever given a name. The absence of any element that would anchor the work to a particular time or place has the effect of making the work universally relatable and thus all the more terrifying. *The Road* earned McCarthy the Pulitzer Prize for Fiction in 2007. *The Road* may not be suitable for younger readers because it contains several scenes that are graphically violent in nature.

AUTHOR BIOGRAPHY

McCarthy was born to Charles Joseph and Gladys Christina McGrail McCarthy on July 20, 1933, in Providence, Rhode Island. Although he was christened Charles, like his father, his name was later legally changed to Cormac. The McCarthy family moved from Rhode Island to Knoxville, Tennessee, in 1937, when the author was four years old.

In 1951, McCarthy began attending the University of Tennessee, majoring in liberal arts. He left in 1953 to join the U.S. Air Force. He spent four years in the air force, half the time stationed in Alaska. He left the air force in 1956 and from 1957 to 1959 returned to his studies at the University of Tennessee. It was during this time that he had two short stories published in the school's literary magazine, *The Phoenix*: "A Drowning Incident" and "Wake for Susan." For his efforts, he earned the university's Ingram-Merrill Award for creative writing in both 1959 and 1960.

After leaving college, McCarthy moved to Chicago, where he worked as an auto mechanic and continued to pursue creative writing. In 1961, he married Lee Holleman, a fellow writer. The couple returned to Sevier County, Tennessee, and had a son named Cullen. Holleman and McCarthy later divorced.

In 1965, McCarthy received a traveling

fellowship from the American Academy of Arts and Letters. He used the money to travel to Europe. On an ocean liner crossing the Atlantic, he met Anne DeLisle, a woman he would marry the following year. Later in 1965, McCarthy's first novel, *The Orchard Keeper*, was published. While his novel was hitting bookstores for the first time and receiving positive reviews, McCarthy and Anne traveled around Europe together, eventually settling in Ibiza, a Mediterranean island off the coast of Spain. It was there that McCarthy completed his second novel, *Outer Dark*, which was published to critical acclaim in 1968.

In 1968, McCarthy and Anne left Europe and moved into a house in Rockford, Tennessee. They later divorced. The following year, he received the Guggenheim Fellowship for Creative Writing and moved to the outskirts of Louisville, Tennessee. Over the next several years McCarthy continued to write and publish his works. His novel *Child of God* was published in 1973; he wrote the screenplay for a PBS film called The *Gardener's Son*, which premiered in 1978; and his fourth novel, *Suttre*, was published in 1979. In 1981, he received a MacArthur Fellowship.

Over the next several decades, McCarthy produced his most notable works to date. Although *Blood Meridian* did not receive much notice upon its publication in 1985, critics would later deem it one of McCarthy's strongest works and possibly even one of the greatest works of American fiction. It made *Time* magazine's list of the one hundred best English-language books published between 1923 and 2005. *Blood Meridian*, and most of McCarthy's subsequent works, are heavily grounded in the southern gothic and western traditions, meaning that they employ dark, grotesque, and sometimes supernatural elements and take place in the southern and western United States.

The first volume of McCarthy's "Border Trilogy," *All the Pretty Horses*, was published by Knopf in 1992. It was the first of McCarthy's novels to be widely read, becoming a New York Times bestseller within the first six months of its publication. The work earned McCarthy a National Book Award and a National Book Critics Circle Award and was the first of his works to be adapted as a major motion picture. Other works of McCarthy's that have been adapted to film are *No Country for Old Men* and *The Road*.

Published in 2006, *The Road* has garnered much praise. In the year of its publication it received the James Tait Black Memorial Prize for Fiction and the Believer Book Award. It also received the 2007 Pulitzer Prize for Fiction. McCarthy is notorious for being protective of his privacy and does not frequently give interviews. As of 2011, McCarthy lived with his third wife, Jennifer Winkley, and their son, John.

PLOT SUMMARY

The Road is not broken into chapters or parts, but rather is written as a single, undivided narrative. Occasionally, the author uses three-dot ellipses to signify a change in the narrative.

As the novel opens, an omniscient narrator describes a man reaching out to touch a young boy in the woods somewhere in the middle of the night. The man is simply referred to as "he," and the boy is called "the child." Throughout the novel, these characters will remain nameless, most frequently being called "the man" and "the boy." The man, having just woken suddenly from a strange dream, checks to make sure the boy is still breathing.

The next morning the man rises while the boy is still sleeping and surveys the surrounding landscape. It is described as "barren, silent, godless." The man is not sure what month of the year it is, although winter is approaching, and he and the boy are headed south to avoid the cold. Their exact location is never revealed, although it is somewhere in the United States. The man looks at the landscape again. It is gray and bleak, with nothing on the horizon. Evidently they are in a lifeless place, void of any inhabitants or vegetation. The man begins preparing some breakfast for himself and the boy from supplies they are carrying along with them in a grocery cart. When they boy finally wakes he says, "Hi, Papa," and it becomes evident that the man and child are father and son.

MEDIA ADAPTATIONS

- An adaptation of *The Road* as an audio-book, read by Tom Stechschulte, was produced and distributed by Recorded Books in 2006.

- *The Road*, adapted as a film by John Hillcoat, starring Viggo Mortensen, Charlize Theron, and Kodi Smit-McPhee, was produced by Dimension Films, 2929 Productions, Nick Wechsler Productions, and Chockstone Pictures in 2009. It is available as a DVD from Sony Pictures Home Entertainment (2010).

The man and the boy set out along a road, pushing the cart with them. The way the surroundings have been described up to this point hints that the setting is sometime in the future, after some catastrophic event has ravaged the earth, wiping out most of human civilization. The man and the boy come to an old abandoned gas station along the road and stop to look for things that might be useful. They do not find much. They continue along the road until the man suddenly realizes that there may be oil remnants in discarded oil bottles in the trash cans back at the gas station. They go back to the gas station to dig through the trash, discover that the man's hunch was correct, and consolidate the small amounts of oil left in the bottoms of the discarded bottles into one to use as fuel for fires. They continue again.

Soon it begins to rain. They stop and cover themselves with a tarp to stay dry. When the rain stops they make camp for the night. The boy asks his father if they are going to die, but the father reassures the boy that they are not dying yet. The father tells the boy that if he, the boy, died, then he, the father, would want to die as well.

The next day they pass through a city and see a dried corpse on the side of the road. The man does not want the boy to see it because "the things you put into your head are there forever."

When the man wakes one day he hears thunder and worries that it might rain. He thinks that if it rains, he and the boy will die because they are in a part of the country where there are no supplies to make a fire to dry by.

The narrator tells us that the man often dreams of his wife, but he distrusts these dreams. He thinks about her during the day as well. The man and the boy eventually come to the city that the man is from and find the house that he grew up in.

They enter the house and explore. The man shows the boy where he used to sleep, but the boy becomes scared and they leave. The narrator tells us that it has been some years since the event that has wiped the earth happened and that there used to be many refugees but now there are few. The man and the boy must pass through mountains to get to the southern coast they are headed toward, but the man is not sure if they will have enough food.

The man gives the boy some hot cocoa, but the boy scolds him for not taking half for himself. The boy does not want his father to sacrifice his own portion of their food stores for his sake.

The man and the boy camp near a river. The man knows that they cannot stay by the river for long, because the water will attract other travelers who might be dangerous. In the world they live in, every day is a fight for survival, and no one can be trusted.

They come upon a bridge obscured by a large truck and trailer. The man looks into the trailer and sees many dried corpses. They continue on, eventually reaching a patch of road that is very hot, and surrounded by charred and smoking trees. They conclude that a forest fire must have swept through a few hours before their arrival. Because the asphalt is melted and too hot to walk on, they make camp for the night to allow the road time to cool.

In the morning, they see tracks in the road. They eventually come upon the man who left them, a charred man with one eye burned shut. The man explains to the boy that the burned man has been struck by lightning. The boy wants to help the burned man, but his father pushes on, explaining that there is nothing they can do for him.

The man abandons his one photograph of his wife in the road. At night he remembers the day of the unspecified catastrophic event. There was a long flash of light and several booms. The power went out instantly.

When the boy wakes he says he wishes that he were with his mother, meaning that he wishes he were dead. The man has a flashback to the day that his wife died. The man and his wife had an argument, in which he begged her not to commit suicide. She claimed that they have nothing left to live for, and if it were not for the man she would kill her son before killing herself. She was certain that if they stay alive, sooner or later they will be caught by other humans, raped, murdered, and eaten. The man begged her not to do it, for his sake and for the boy's sake, but she would not be persuaded. She went into the darkness and killed herself with an obsidian rock.

One morning, the man is woken by a noise and looks up to see a roving band of men, wearing masks and carrying weapons, accompanied by a diesel truck. The man urges the boy to run, and they get as far away as possible. The truck stops and one of the men walks towards them. When the man sees them, the father threatens him with the gun they carry. It only has two bullets. When the man from the truck grabs the boy, the boy's father uses one of the bullets to shoot the man in the head, splattering the man's brains all over the boy. They run far and fast.

The man explains to the boy that even though he killed a man, they are still the "good guys," because he had to do it for the boy's protection.

One day, the man has a feeling that they are being watched. They see another little boy, and the boy calls to him. The man's son calls out to the boy, but the man scolds him, and the boy cries. They move on, but the boy continues to lament the fact that they left the other boy behind. They eat the last of their food stores and make camp.

In the morning, the man is woken by a band of travelers marching along the road. The man and the boy crouch low to hide. The travelers are all wearing red and carrying pipes wrapped in leather for weapons. The boy asks his father if they are bad guys, and the man confirms that they are.

Eventually the snowdrifts become so high that they are forced to abandon their shopping cart, taking only what they can carry.

The man and the boy come upon a large, stately house. The man decides to investigate the house against his better judgment because they have had no food for five days and are starving.

The house appears to be inhabited. They do not find any food in the kitchen, so the man decides to break into the locked cellar in search of goods. The boy is terrified and begs him not to, but eventually they descend the cellar steps together. What they find is a horrific scene: a man lays on a bloody mattress, his legs cut off at the hip, while other people cower against the back wall naked, squinting, and pleading for help. The man and the boy flee up the stairs immediately. From the kitchen they can see four men and two women coming back toward the house, evidently its inhabitants, who captured the people in the basement and keep them as a source of food. The man and the boy run and hide in the field behind the house. The man contemplates whether, if it came to it, he would be able to kill his son to save him from being captured, murdered, and eaten.

Several days later, back on the road, the boy, upset, asks his father, "We wouldn't ever eat anybody, would we?" His father reassures him that they would not, even if they were starving, because they are the good guys.

Later the man and the boy come upon a single house in a field. After exploring the backyard, the man discovers the door to a storm cellar, covered with dirt. The boy is frightened and begs the man not to go in, but the man eventually convinces him that it is all right to go inside.

Inside, the man is ecstatically shocked to discover a fully stocked shelter, replete with hundreds of canned goods, gallons of water, blankets, a portable stove, and much more. They stay in the shelter for several days, eating well and resting. When it is time to leave, they pack the stove and as many canned goods as possible in a new grocery cart that they found at the last town.

On the road again, they spot a man ahead of them. They catch up with him and discover him to be a hunched elderly man, who is filthy, smelly, and wary of them. The boy persuades his father to let the man camp with them for the night and have some of their food.

The old man is very philosophical about life and death and speaks in strange, invented truisms. In the morning, they part ways. The man is getting progressively sicker, coughing more and more frequently. He believes that he is dying and worries about leaving his child.

After camping in a field one night, the man wakes up weak with fever. His cough becomes almost constant, and the boy becomes afraid that his father is going to die.

As they travel on, the man continues to get weaker. They pass the corpses of a group of people who had been burned alive.

One day the boy spots campfire smoke ahead of them. The man decides that they should sneak close enough to take a look, to determine whether the people making the fire are a danger. When they find the clearing where the people had camped, it is deserted. The others heard the man and the boy approaching, saw that they had a gun, and fled. As they get closer to their camp, they see a charred human infant gutted and roasting over the fire.

Several days later, the boy spots a house far in the distance. They travel to the house and find some canned goods in the kitchen. The man thinks the goods had not been discovered yet because the house was nearly impossible to see from the road. They camp at the house for four days eating and resting. They pack their cart with as much food as possible and continue on toward the coast. Eventually, they spot the ocean on the horizon and an hour later arrive at the beach. The boy insists on going swimming in the freezing-cold ocean water. They camp for a night and then travel down the coast until they spot a ship stuck out in the waves.

The man swims out to see if there is anything useful on the ship. He finds some tools and cans of food.

The man transports as much as possible back to the beach in a tarp. They start to travel back to their campsite but after some distance realize that the boy left their pistol in the sand by the ship. They have to go back for it. After finding the gun, they head toward their campsite again, but night falls before they make it back. They continue on in the blackness.

They finally make it back to their campsite. The next morning they spend several hours unloading more supplies from the ship. The man finds a flare gun aboard, among other things. The next day the boy wakes with a fever. The man gives him some medicine that he found on the ship and tries to comfort him as much as he is able. The boy sleeps all day.

The next day the boy feels better. They go exploring on the beach again. However, on the way back to their campsite, they are troubled to notice boot prints in the sand. When they get back to their campsite they find that everything has been stolen. They hastily take off in pursuit of the thief, following his tracks. When they come upon him, the boy's father levels the gun at him and demands that he step back from the cart. The thief, threatened by the gun, obeys. The boy's father then demands that the thief strip naked, pile his clothes on the cart, and walk away. The thief pleads with him, but the boy's father explains that he is going to leave the man the way that the man left the boy and his son after stealing their possessions: with nothing. After the thief leaves, at the urging of the boy they call for him in an attempt to return his clothes, but he does not answer. They travel on, eventually making their way to an abandoned port town.

As they pass through the town, an arrow suddenly comes flying at them, piercing the man's leg. They look up to see that they are being attacked from an upstairs window of one of the buildings. The man reacts quickly, shooting the flare gun up at the window and setting the room from which the arrow came on fire. They move on to a safe place where the man can suture his leg. Two days later they leave the town.

They continue to travel, and the man's cough continues to worsen. He is now coughing up large quantities of blood.

After more traveling, they head inland. The man, too weak to go any farther, lies down knowing that he will not get back up. The next morning the man tells the boy to leave him, take the pistol, and keep walking. The boy pleads with the man to get up. The man tells him that he cannot, but that the boy must continue on, doing everything as they have been doing. The man tells him to always carry the fire and never take any chances. He tells the boy that even after he is dead the boy will still be able to talk to him in his imagination.

The man sleeps most of the rest of the day and the night. When the boy wakes in the morning, his father is dead beside him. He sobs over his body and stays next to it for three days. Eventually he walks back to the road and sees someone approaching. He waits, gun in hand, in the road for the man to approach. The man is wearing a yellow ski parka and carrying a gun. He asks the boy several questions about the man he was with, and when the boy explains that the man was his father and now is dead, the man in the yellow parka urges the boy to come along with him. The man assures the boy that he is one of the good guys. When the boy asks for proof, the man answers that he has none, and the boy will have to take a gamble.

The man tells the boy that he has a family of his own, a wife, a son, and a daughter. The boy asks the man whether he eats people, to which the man responds that he does not. After saying good-bye to his father, the boy goes with the man. When the little boy meets the man's wife, she embraces him and says that she is happy to see him. The narrator explains that sometimes the woman would talk to the boy about God. The boy was not able to talk to God the way the woman wanted, but he was able to talk to his father, and he never forgot him

The final paragraph of the book is a poetic meditation on life on earth prior to the apocalypse and prior to its habitation and destruction by man.

CHARACTERS

The Boy

The boy is one of the two protagonists of the novel, the other being the man. The narrator never provides explicit facts or details about the boy or the man, but much can be inferred from their actions. The boy is most likely under the age of ten. He is too young to remember much of the world before the catastrophic event occurred, so he seems to take life as it is without lamenting what has been lost. The boy is frequently described as being very thin, small, frail, and white. He is often terrified of their surroundings and wary of other people and the enclosed spaces that they might hide in. The boy is selfless and filled with love for his father, his only companion, although he frequently (and correctly) suspects that his father is lying to him to cover up the true direness of their situation.

The boy asks countless questions of his father about the way the world was before the event, about when they are going to die, and other things that he thinks about. Sometimes the boy says that he wishes he were dead, to the great dismay of his father. Although his personality is typical for his age in many ways, he is unusually intuitive and accepting. The boy also has very strong morals. He always wants to help the people they meet along the road and is disappointed when his father refuses.

Because the desperation of their situation sometimes causes the man to do horrific things, such as commit murder, the boy is constantly seeking assurance that they are the good guys, not the bad guys. The boy believes that they are the good guys because, as his father has told him, they are "carrying the fire," although he is not quite sure what that means.

The Boy's Mother

The boy's mother, who is also the man's wife, does not appear in the novel: the man dreams about her and discusses her with the boy. She committed suicide by somehow injuring herself on a piece of obsidian prior to the beginning of the novel. The man thinks of her longingly sometimes but is resolved that her memory can have no place in his life or the boy's because she abandoned them both. Through the man's dreams and flashbacks, the reasons she committed suicide are revealed. She believed her family's capture, rape, and murder by cannibals to be inevitable and that by staying alive they were only prolonging their suffering. One night, despite the man's pleading, she walked into the woods and killed herself.

The Elderly Man

The boy and his father come across the elderly man on the road one day. The man is filthy and hunched and can barely see. At the boy's request, the father allows the elderly man to camp with them for a night and have some of their food. The elderly man proclaims that there is no God. He does not thank the boy for the food, because as he sees it the food will only prolong the time that he has to dread his imminent death. After camping together for one night, the man and the boy part ways with the elderly man. They both know that he is going to die.

The Man

The man is one of the two protagonists of the novel, the other being the boy. The narrator never provides explicit facts or details about the boy or the man, but much can be inferred from their actions. The man is the father of the boy. Unlike his wife, the man is filled with an inexplicable urge to live and to protect the life of his son at all costs. The boy is all that matters to the man, his "world entire." Everything that the man does, he does for the boy. Although the man is fighting for survival for himself and the boy, he is not sure why. He was not even able to convince his wife not to commit suicide, because, as he admits, he could not think of a good reason for her not to. However, he tells the boy that they must not ever give up, and they must continue to "carry the fire," because that is what the good guys do. The man is clever and resourceful, able to find food where others had overlooked it. He is nearly always patient with the boy. He tries to tell the boy stories and do other things for his amusement.

The Man from the Truck

When a truck breaks down on the side of the road near where the man and the boy are camped, a man from the truck heads in their direction to relieve himself in the woods. Although the father and boy try to hide, the man comes upon their hiding spot. He urges them to join him and the rest of the travelers with the truck, but the boy's father knows that they are cannibals and that the man is trying to capture them for food. When the man from the truck grabs the boy, the boy's father shoots the man in the head, killing him instantly.

The Man in the Yellow Parka

At the end of the novel, after the boy's father has died, a man in a yellow parka approaches the little boy and asks him if he would like to join his family. The boy questions him, and the man answers that he is one of the good guys, he is not a cannibal, and he has children of his own. The boy decides to go with the man.

The Man Who Shot the Arrow

When the man and the boy are passing through a port town near the ocean the man is shot in the leg by an arrow from a man in the window of a two-story building. The man who shot the arrow was attempting to kill the man and his son to rob them and potentially eat them.

The Man's Wife

See The Boy's Mother

The Naked People

When the man and the boy break into the cellar of an old colonial house looking for food, they find many naked people locked within. The people have been captured by the inhabitants of the house, who are going to eat them for sustenance.

The Other Little Boy

Along the road the man and the boy catch a brief glimpse of another little boy. The son begs his father to let the other little boy come along with them. The man refuses, claiming that the boy has parents, and they are just hiding. It is clear that the son greatly sympathizes with the other little boy. At several points throughout the rest of the novel, the son asks his father if he thinks the other little boy is all right and laments the fact that they did not bring him with them.

TOPICS FOR FURTHER STUDY

- In the barren world in which *The Road* is set, many of the characters seem to have different ideas regarding the meaning of life and of their suffering. Consider the viewpoints of the boy, the man, and the elderly man regarding life, death, and God. What branch of philosophy or religion do each of their viewpoints seem most closely aligned with? If you are unsure, use the Internet to research terms such as Christianity, determinism, existentialism, and nihilism. Write a paragraph about each of the three characters explaining their belief systems. Support your assertions

with evidence from the text and your
research.

- Read the young-adult novel *Life as
We Knew It* (Harcourt Children's
Books, 2006) by Susan Beth Pfeffer.
The characters in *Life as We Knew It*
deal with extreme weather changes
and food shortages following an
apocalyptic event, similar to the
experiences of the man and the boy
in *The Road*. How do the plights of
the characters in both works
compare? Psychologically, how do
the characters deal with trauma?
Write an essay compiling your
findings.

- In *The Road*, the man and the boy
suffer from poor nutrition and
starvation, which debilitates them
mentally and physically. At one
point, the man worries that if he
does not find vitamin D, the boy will
get rickets. Using the Internet,
research the FDA guidelines for
proper health and nutrition for both
adolescent boys and adult men.
Create a PowerPoint presentation
educating your classmates about an
aspect of good nutrition, including
the importance of vitamins.

- Watch the 2009 film adaptation of
The Road (DVD, Sony Pictures

Home Entertainment, 2010). Do you think that the adaptation was an accurate representation of the literary work? In a small group with several other classmates, use a camera and video-editing software such as iMovie to create your own film adaptation of a scene from *The Road*. Post it and links to the original scene on your Web page and invite classmates to discuss which representation is best.

The Thief

One day while the man and the boy are away from their campsite on the beach, a thief steals all of their belongings. They are able to track him down by his boot prints and the trail of sand he left behind. When they find him, the father demands that he strip naked and walk away from their things, leaving his clothes behind. The thief begs the man not to make him strip, but the man says that they are going to leave the thief the same way that the thief left them when he stole their things: with nothing.

The Wife of the Man in the Yellow Parka

At the end of the novel, when the boy joins the family of the man with the yellow parka, he meets the man's wife. She hugs the boy and tells him she is happy to see him. After the boy joins her family, she often talks to him about God.

THEMES

Love

The most prominent theme in *The Road* is that of love. The man's love for the boy and his hope for the boy's survival are what sustain him and what propel him to keep moving forward. The man's love for the boy is so overwhelming that in his eyes the boy is perfect, infallible, nearly divine. In fact, the man compares him to a god as early as the third paragraph in the novel: "[The man] knew only that the child was his warrant. He said: If he is not the word of God God never spoke." The man's love for the boy is so powerful that it renders him not merely his son but his savior. To the man, his love for his son makes existence worthwhile.

Survival

Survival is one of the most obvious themes in the work. For the man and the boy, every single day is a fight for survival. The man's will for survival is constant, although he is unable to justify it or explain where it comes from. The man's will to survive is starkly contrasted with the lack of a will to survive in both his wife and his son. Before his wife takes her own life he begs her not to do it, but she argues that they have no reason to continue living, no reason to fight for survival, and he is unable to list one single reason why she should. He admits, "She was right. There was no argument." However, for some reason he has a will to keep going. He tells his son, "This is what the good guys do. They keep trying. They dont give up."

Frequently throughout the book the man tells his son that they are "carrying the fire." The fire that he refers to could be understood as a metaphor for the inexplicable will to live that burns inside of him. At the end of the novel, when the man is dying and his son begs him to let him die with him the man responds: "You cant. You have to carry the fire. … It's inside you. It was always there. I can see it."

Good and Evil

Despite the fact that the novel is set in an apocalyptic world, the man and the boy still maintain a moral code and are careful to clearly delineate between good and evil. Notions of good and evil surface frequently throughout the work, because the young boy is preoccupied with making sure that they are "good guys." The bad guys, of course, are those who have given up on morality. The bad guys travel in roving bands, torturing and raping those that they come across. The bad guys either keep their prisoners as slaves or murder them and eat them.

The innocent boy is the epitome of goodness. He always wants to help everyone that they come across, even if it means diminishing his own chances of survival by sharing their food and shelter. Sometimes the boy is critical of the fact that his father does not want to help others. Whenever his father commits an act of violence or neglects to help someone in need, the boy asks him if they are still the good guys, seeking reassurance. At the end of the novel when the man is dying, he provides his son with the ultimate reassurance: "You're the best guy. You always were."

STYLE

Dystopian Novel

The Road is an example of a dystopian novel, meaning that it depicts life, sometime in the future, in a society that would be undesirable to live in. The term *dystopia* comes from the Greek word for "bad place," and it is the opposite of the Greek word *utopia*, which means good place. Usually in dystopian novels, the world has degenerated as a result of the mistakes or poor judgment of mankind. Frequently, writers of dystopian fiction seek to warn against a future that could become reality if mankind does not alter its course of action.

The Road can be categorized as a dystopian novel because it is set in the future and depicts a horrific society in which day-to-day life consists of scavenging for any edible morsel and hiding from bands of cannibals on the hunt for flesh. The landscape is barren; virtually everything remotely beautiful has been wiped away. The world depicted in *The Road* is so awful that the man's wife committed suicide to escape it, and even the man admits that he does not have a reason to live, though he cannot escape his will to. Although it is not clear whether the catastrophic event that created this new landscape was caused by man, the description in the novel leads the reader to believe it was most likely some sort of nuclear explosion.

Punctuation

Minimal punctuation is one of the most distinctive and recognizable elements of McCarthy's writing style, not just in *The Road* but in many of his novels. In *The Road*, McCarthy never uses quotation marks to identify dialogue or for any other purpose. This is very unusual for contemporary fiction. Sometimes lines of dialogue are set apart by a new line, but sometimes an entire conversation between two characters will happen on one line, without any quotation marks or line breaks. This forces the reader to pay closer attention to the dialogue in the novel, because it is easy to lose track of who is speaking unless you have a grasp of the rhythm of the conversation that is happening.

McCarthy rarely uses other forms of punctuation as well. He uses short, declarative sentences that most often do not require any punctuation other than a period. Colons, semicolons, ellipses, and even apostrophes are hard to find in *The Road*.

HISTORICAL CONTEXT

The Road is set in the future on the planet Earth. Most critics and reviewers of the work have assumed that it takes place on the eastern coast of the United States, based on descriptions in the work of the geography and terrain that the man and the boy traverse. Although it can only be speculated, it is probable that the cultural and political climate of the early twenty-first century inspired McCarthy to write a work of dystopian fiction, either in a subconscious or purposeful way. Dystopian works often reflect what the the author views as a version of the future that is unpleasant but likely to become reality if mankind continues to evolve along its current trajectory. Therefore, although they portray events of the future, dystopian novels can sometimes be interpreted as a social commentary on the cultural, social, and political atmosphere in which the work was written.

In a televised interview with Oprah Winfrey on the *Oprah Winfrey Show* (McCarthy's only nonprint interview, as of 2011), McCarthy stated that in the wake of the attacks of September 11, 2001, a climate of fear and preoccupation with apocalyptic events in the United States spread. The events to which McCarthy referred in the interview were the series of terrorist suicide attacks on the United States that occurred on September 11, 2001, just five years before the publication of the novel. On that day, terrorist operatives from the militant

Islamist group al-Qaeda hijacked and crashed four American passenger planes, killing nearly three thousand people. Two of the hijacked planes were flown into the World Trade Center towers in New York City, and one was flown into the Pentagon in Arlington, Virginia. The fourth plane crashed into a field in Shanksville, Pennsylvania, after passengers on the aircraft attempted to take control of it before it hit its intended target in Washington, D.C. After much speculation, al-Qaeda leader Osama bin Laden admitted responsibility for the attacks. U.S. support of Israel, implementation of sanctions against Iraq, and the presence of U.S. troops in Saudi Arabia were all listed by al-Qaeda and bin Laden as reasons for the attacks.

The United States responded to the attacks by initiating a so-called war on terror. The goal of the war on terror was to locate and eliminate members of al-Qaeda and other known terrorist sects and bring about the fall of the Taliban (a militant Islamist political group). As of 2011, America was still engaged in war in Afghanistan. Certainly, living in a country saturated with the fear of terrorism and the threat of modern nuclear warfare could, in part, have inspired McCarthy to write *The Road*.

CRITICAL OVERVIEW

The Road was published in 2006 to much critical acclaim. Reviewers of the work almost unanimously agree that it is unavoidably affecting. In a review called "The Road through Hell, Paved with Desperation," printed in the *New York Times*, contributor Janet Maslin lauded the novel:

> *The Road* would be pure misery if not for its stunning, savage beauty. This is an exquisitely bleak incantation—pure poetic brimstone. Mr. McCarthy has summoned his fiercest visions to invoke the devastation. … *The Road* offers nothing in the way of escape or comfort. But its fearless wisdom is more indelible than reassurance could ever be.

In a review of the work called "The Road to Hell," printed in the London *Guardian*, contributor Alan Warner commented,

> *The Road* affirms belief in the tender pricelessness of the here and now. In creating an exquisite nightmare, it does not add to the cruelty and ugliness of our times; it warns us how much we have to lose. It makes the novels of the contemporary Savants seem infantile and horribly

over-rated. Beauty and goodness are here aplenty and we should think about them. While we can.

In the *Hudson Review*, reviewer Alan Davis attributed the success of *The Road* to McCarthy's writing prowess in his essay "Apocalypse Now": "Were it not for McCarthy's mythmaking prose, the book itself rather than its milieu would be a disaster."

One of McCarthy's most widely read books to date, *The Road* was further popularized when, on March 28, 2007, it was named as a book selection for Oprah's Book Club. That same year it was awarded the Pulitzer Prize for Fiction.

There has been ample critical debate concerning whether or not the work represents a departure from McCarthy's usual style. In "'Maps of the World in Its Becoming': Post-Apocalyptic Naming in Cormac McCarthy's *The Road*," in the *Journal of Modern Literature*, contributor Ashley Kunsa states,

> We cannot traverse *The Road* without a startling awareness of its departure from McCarthy's previous style. Along with its odd approach to naming, the fractured narrative structure, proliferation of sentence fragments, and brief, repetitive dialogue differentiate the novel from the rest of his work.

Yet in a review of the critical text *No Place for*

Home: Spatial Constraint and Character Flight in the Novels of Cormac McCarthy published in the *Rocky Mountain Review*, Craig Monk claims that "for all its horror and bleakness, no one could argue that *The Road* represents a radical departure for McCarthy." Only time will tell whether the book will continue to be widely read and praised and whether it truly stands apart from the rest of his body of work.

SOURCES

"All-Time 100 Novels," in *Time*, http://www.time.com/time/specials/packages/comple (accessed September 23, 2011).

Banco, Lindsey, "Contractions in Cormac McCarthy's *The Road*," in *Explicator*, Vol. 68, No. 4, 2010, pp. 276–79.

Boog, Jason, "Oprah Winfrey Closes Her TV Book Club," in *GalleyCat*, May 25, 2011, http://www.mediabistro.com/galleycat/top-10-bestselling-books-in-oprahs-book-club_b30637 (accessed September 23, 2011).

"Cormac McCarthy: A Biography," in *Cormac McCarthy.com*, http://www.cormacmccarthy.com/Biography.htm (accessed September 5, 2011).

"Cormac McCarthy Biography," in *Biography.com*, http://www.biography.com/articles/CormacMcCarth 9390745 (accessed September 5, 2011).

Davis, Alan, "Apocalypse Now," Review of *The Road*, in *Hudson Review*, Vol. 60, No. 1, Spring 2007, pp. 145–50.

DeBruyn, Ben, "Borrowed Time, Borrowed World, and Borrowed Eyes: Care, Ruin, and Vision in McCarthy's *The Road* and Harrison's Ecocriticism," in *English Studies*, Vol. 91, No. 7, October 2010, pp. 776–89.

"Dystopia," in *The Bedford Glossary of Critical and Literary Terms*, edited by Ross Murfin and Supriya M. Ray, Bedford/St. Martin's Press, 2003, p. 122.

Grindly, Carl James, "The Setting of McCarthy's *The Road*," in *Explicator*, Vol. 67, No. 1, Fall 2008, pp. 11–13.

Kunsa, Ashley, "'Maps of the World in Its Becoming': Post-Apocalyptic Naming in Cormac McCarthy's *The Road*," in *Journal of Modern Literature*, Vol. 33, No. 1, Fall 2009, pp. 57–74.

Maslin, Janet, "The Road through Hell, Paved with Desperation," Review of *The Road*, in *New York Times*, September 25, 2006, p. E1.

McCarthy, Cormac, *The Road*, Vintage Books, 2007.

Monk, Craig, Review of *No Place for Home: Spatial Constraint and Character Flight in the Novels of Cormac McCarthy*, in *Rocky Mountain Review*, Vol. 62, No. 1, Spring 2008, pp. 109–10.

Rambo, Shelly L., "Beyond Redemption? Reading Cormac McCarthy's *The Road* after the End of the World," in *Studies in the Literary Imagination*, Vol. 41, No. 2, Fall 2008, pp. 99–120.

Warner, Alan, "The Road to Hell," Review of *The Road*, in *Guardian* (London, England), November 3, 2006.

FURTHER READING

Hall, Juliette, *Essential Authors: Cormac McCarthy*, Webster's Digital Services, 2011.

> Hall's book places the work of McCarthy within the context of American literature and provides an overview of the author's most important influences, styles, and themes. This book provides a solid introduction to McCarthy for those who are unfamiliar with his work.

Heffernan, Teresa, *Post-apocalyptic Culture*: Modernism, *Postmodernism, and the Twentieth-Century Novel*, University of Toronto Press, 2008.

> Heffernan's book provides insight into the cultural reasons behind the viewpoints of many of the characters in *The Road* regarding the fact that the near extinction of humanity is upon them. According to Heffernan, in contemporary culture people largely view a potential apocalypse to be a catastrophic event, although this has not always been the case.

McCarthy, William, *Postmodern Literature and Its Writers: A Look at Cormac McCarthy, Don DeLillo, Thomas Pynchon, and Paul Auster*, Webster's Digital Services, 2011.

In this work, the author provides an overview of postmodern literature, addressing the works of McCarthy and several of his contemporaries. The book includes readings and analyses of McCarthy's writing.

Stroud, Les, *Will to Live: Dispatches from the Edge of Survival*, Harper Paperbacks, 2011.

In this book, Stroud, creator of the television show *Survivorman*, explains how humans deal with life-or-death situations. Using many real-life examples, Stroud explains how people find the will to fight for survival when all seems lost. This work provides insight into the experience of the man in *The Road* and his fight to keep himself and his son alive.

SUGGESTED SEARCH TERMS

Cormac McCarthy

Cormac McCarthy AND The Road

Cormac McCarthy AND postmodernis

The Road AND postmodernism

The Road AND apocalypse

Cormac McCarthy AND nihilism

Cormac McCarthy AND style

The Road AND style

The Road AND meaning of life

The Road AND dystopian novel

CPSIA information can be obtained
at www.ICGtesting.com
Printed in the USA
BVHW08s0243290618
520331BV00013B/490/P

9 781375 397261